MW00979877

The Precious Blood of Christ

WITNESS LEE

LIVING STREAM MINISTRY
Anaheim, California • www.lsm.org

ISBN 978-1-57593-986-5

Living Stream Ministry
2431 W. Ball Road, Anaheim, CA 92801
P. O. Box 2121, Anaheim, CA 92814 USA

Printed in India

11 12 13 14 15 / 15 14 13 12 11 10

THE PRECIOUS BLOOD OF CHRIST

To sustain your physical life, you need certain basic items such as water, oxygen, food, clothing, and shelter. In addition, your body requires a certain amount of protein, vitamins, and minerals. Without all these, your physical life would die, or at least suffer greatly.

It is the same with your spiritual life. Your spiritual life, just like your physical life, requires certain basic elements. These are essential. Without them, you will find it difficult to survive as a Christian in a world that does not know Christ. One of these basic elements is the blood of Christ.

Why do you need the blood of Christ? Because, essentially, fallen man has three basic problems. Even as a Christian, you still carry around the fallen human life. So day after day, you may still be plagued with these three problems.

These three problems involve three

parties: God, yourself, and Satan. Toward God, you often sense separation. Within yourself, you often sense guilt. And from Satan, you often sense accusation. These three—separation from God, feelings of guilt, and accusation from Satan—can be three big problems in your Christian life. How can these be overcome? Only by the blood of Christ.

SEPARATION FROM GOD

When Adam sinned in the garden of Eden, he immediately hid from God. Before Adam sinned, he enjoyed God and was in His presence all the time. Yet after he sinned, he hid. Sin always results in separation from God.

Even as a Christian you may experience this. After committing some little sin, you sense a great gulf between you and God. Because God is righteous, He cannot tolerate sins. This is what the prophet Isaiah said: "No, Jehovah's hand is not so short that it cannot save; / Nor is His ear so heavy that it cannot hear. / But your iniquities have become a separation / Between you and your God, / And your sins have hidden His face / From you so that He does not hear" (Isa. 59:1-2).

After Adam sinned, God did not say, "Adam, what have you done?" Rather, God said, "Adam, where are you?" In other words, God is not as much concerned with what sins you may commit, as He is with the fact that your sins separate you from Him. God loves you, but He abhors your sins. As long as your sins remain, God must stay away. In this condition, you feel far from God. For God to come, sins must go.

There is only one thing in the entire universe that can take away sins—the precious blood of Christ. No amount of prayer, no amount of weeping, no ritual, no penance, no promise to do better, no guilty feeling, no period of waiting—no, nothing but the precious blood of Christ—can remove sins. Hebrews 9:22 says that "without shedding of blood is no forgiveness."

This is illustrated in Exodus. Some of the children of Israel may have been as sinful as the Egyptians. Yet when God sent His angel to slay all the firstborn

3

children in the land of Egypt, He did not say, "When I see your good behavior, I will pass over you." God did not require that the children of Israel pray, do penance, or promise to behave. No, God commanded them to slay the Passover lamb and to sprinkle its blood on their doorposts. He said, "When I see the blood, I will pass over you" (Exo. 12:13). God never looked to see what kind of people were in the house; when He saw the blood, He simply passed over.

That Passover lamb was a picture of Christ. When John the Baptist first saw the Lord he proclaimed, "Behold, the Lamb of God, who takes away the sin of the world!" (John 1:29). Jesus is the Lamb of God. By His precious blood all your sins have been taken away.

What then should you do when you have sinned and feel far from God? You should simply confess that sin to God and believe that the blood of Jesus has taken that sin away. First John 1:9 says, "If we confess our sins, He is faithful and righteous to forgive us our sins and cleanse us from all unrighteousness." When you confess your sins, immediately all distance between you and God is gone.

Don't worry about any feeling or lack of feeling at this point. The blood of Christ is primarily for God's satisfaction, not for yours. Remember, God said, "When I (not you) see the blood...." On the night of the Passover, the children of Israel were within the house while the blood of the lamb was without. Within the house, they could not see the blood; nevertheless, they had peace through knowing that God was satisfied with that blood.

Once a year, on the day of atonement, the high priest went alone into the Holy of Holies to sprinkle the blood on the expiation cover of the ark (Lev. 16:11-17). No one was allowed to watch. This is a shadow of Christ who, after His resurrection, went into the heavenly tabernacle and sprinkled His own blood before God as the propitiation for your sins (Heb. 9:12). No one today can look into heaven and see that blood. Yet it is there. It is there speaking for you (Heb. 12:24) and satisfying God on your behalf. Even though you cannot see the blood, you can believe in its effectiveness. This blood solves your problem toward God.

If God esteems the blood of Christ sufficient to remove your sins, can you do the same? Or do you require some good feeling besides? Can your requirement be higher than God's? No, you must simply confess, "O God, thank You that the blood of Christ has taken away all my sins. If You are happy with the blood, then I am happy also."

GUILT IN YOUR CONSCIENCE

Man's second crucial problem is with himself. Within him, in his conscience, there is a heavy load of guilt. How many young people today are burdened by guilt! Guilt is a big problem to man.

Sins offend God on the one hand and defile us on the other. What is guilt? Guilt is the stain of sins on your conscience. When you are young, your conscience is only stained a little. But as you grow older, these stains accumulate. Like a window which is never washed, the conscience grows darker and darker until eventually little light can penetrate.

No detergent, no chemical, no acid can wash the stain of guilt from your conscience. Not even a nuclear bomb can dislodge this stain; no, your conscience demands something more powerful than that. Your conscience needs the precious blood of Christ.

Hebrews 9:14 says, "How much more will the blood of Christ...purify our conscience from dead works to serve the living God?" The blood of Christ is powerful enough to purge, or cleanse, your conscience from every guilty stain.

How does the blood of Christ purge guilt from your conscience? Suppose you receive a traffic ticket for parking on the sidewalk. You have three problems: first, you broke the law; second, you owe the government a fine; and third, you have a copy of the traffic ticket to remind you of the fine. Now suppose you are penniless and find it impossible to pay the fine. You cannot just throw away the ticket, because the police hold a copy, and they will prosecute you if you do not pay. You have a real problem.

This is a picture of what happens

whenever you sin. First, you have broken God's law; that is, you have done something that offends God. Second, you owe God's law something. Romans 6:23 says that the wages of sin is death. This is a rather stiff fine, impossible for you to pay. And third, you have guilt in your conscience, like the traffic ticket in your pocket, as a nagging reminder of your offense.

Now here is the good news. When Jesus Christ died on the cross, His death fully met all the requirements of God's law for you. In other words, your debt of sin has been paid. Praise the Lord! Jesus Christ, through His death on the cross, paid it all!

So now, the first two problems have been solved: God is no longer offended, and the debt of sin has been fully paid. But what about your conscience? The stain of guilt, like the traffic ticket, remains as a record of your sin.

This is where the blood of Christ cleanses your conscience. Because Christ's death has paid the debt of sin, His blood may now wipe out the record of that debt. Just as when the fine is paid, the traffic ticket may be torn up and thrown away, so also any guilt on your conscience may be wiped out.

This is so easy to experience. Whenever you sin and sense guilt within, you may simply open to God and pray something like this: "O God, forgive me for what I did today. Thank You, Lord, on the cross You died for me and paid for this sin that I have committed. Lord, I believe that this sin has been forgiven by You. Right now I claim Your precious blood to cleanse my conscience from any stain of guilt." Remember 1 John 1:9: "If we confess our sins, He is faithful and righteous to forgive us our sins and cleanse us from all unrighteousness." And as Psalm 103:12 says, "As far as the east is from the west, / So far has He removed our transgressions from us." Who can say how far east is from west? In the same way, when you confess your sins, God removes them infinitely far away from you. They are not associated with you anymore. Because of this, you may have rest in your conscience.

When God forgives, He forgets. Do not think that after God has forgiven your sins, He may one day come back and remind you of them again. No, when it comes to your forgiven sins, God has a very short memory. Sometimes you may have a better memory than God. Can God really forget? This is what Jeremiah 31:34 says: "I will forgive their iniquity, and their sin I will remember no more." If God forgets your sins, you may forget them also. Don't remind God of something He has already forgotten.

Christ died nearly two thousand years ago. His blood has already been shed and is available twenty-four hours a day to cleanse your conscience. Whenever you sin, there is no need to wait. Waiting does not improve the power of the blood. The blood is all-powerful. Wherever you are, any time of day, if you sense guilt in your conscience, just claim the precious blood. "Blessed is he whose transgression is forgiven;... / Blessed is the man to whom / Jehovah does not impute iniquity" (Psa. 32:1-2). Through the precious blood of Christ, the problem of guilt is solved.

ACCUSATION FROM SATAN

However, sometimes after you confess and apply the blood you may continue to have some bad feeling within. Does this indicate that your sin is not forgiven? Or that the blood of Christ does not work? Or that something further is needed? You must answer, "Absolutely not!"

Where, then, do these bad feelings come from after you have confessed and applied the blood? Their source is God's enemy, Satan. To understand this we must see who Satan is and what he does.

Satan is the "devil," which in the original language of the Bible means "accuser." So Revelation 12:10 refers to him as "the accuser of our brothers,...who accuses them before our God day and night." Satan, God's enemy, spends most of his time day and night accusing God's people. This is his job. Of course, God did not ask him to do this. Rather, he has taken it upon himself to accuse God's people incessantly.

This is revealed in the story of Job. Job was a righteous man, and feared God (Job 1:1). Yet it is recorded that Satan appeared before God to accuse Job before

Him. He said, "Does Job fear God without cause?...You have blessed the work of his hands, and his possessions are spread throughout the land. But stretch forth Your hand and touch all that he has, and he will surely curse You to Your face" (Job 1:9-11). In other words, Satan accused Job of only fearing God because God had blessed him. Satan claimed that God bribed Job and that if God took away all Job's riches, Job would curse God. This illustrates Satan's accusing in the spiritual realm.

In the book of Zechariah, the high priest, Joshua, stood before God and Satan stood at his right hand "to be his adversary" (3:1). Joshua was "clothed with filthy garments" (v. 3). This speaks of his poor, sinful condition. How often your poor condition gives Satan the opportunity to accuse you. This implies that Satan is not only God's enemy, but he is your enemy as well. Whenever you come to God, Satan resists your coming by accusing you.

Nothing cripples a Christian spiritually more than accusation. Whenever you listen to Satan's accusation, you are powerless. It is as if all the strength is drained from your spirit. A Christian under accusation finds it hard to fellowship with others and even harder to pray. He feels as though he cannot approach God.

This is the enemy's subtlety. He never appears in a red suit with a pitchfork crying, "I am the devil! Now I am going to condemn you!" He is more clever than that. He accuses you inwardly and even tricks you into thinking that his accusations are God's speaking.

How can you distinguish between God's true enlightening in your conscience and Satan's accusation? Sometimes it is difficult, but there are three ways:

First, God's light supplies you, whereas Satan's accusation drains you. When God speaks concerning your sins, you may feel very exposed and wounded. Nevertheless, you are also supplied and encouraged to draw close to God and apply the precious blood of Christ. Satan's accusations, on the other hand, are totally negative. The more you listen, the harder it is to pray. You feel empty and discouraged.

Second, God's speaking is always specific, whereas Satan's condemnation is quite often (though not always) general. Sometimes you may be tricked into thinking that you are just tired, or that you have had a rough day. Other times, you may just have a general impression that you are not right with God. But when you search your conscience, you find no specific sin that would cause you to be separated from God. Or you may wake up with a general feeling of depression or a feeling of uneasiness toward God. All these general feelings of condemnation that have no apparent source in sin are of Satan and should be rejected. When God speaks, He is specific and positive. But when Satan speaks, he is often general and negative.

Third, any uneasy feeling which remains after you confess and claim the blood is of Satan. There is never a need to confess and claim the blood again. God's demand is at once satisfied by the blood. But Satan is never satisfied. He would

14

like to see you confess again and again. Proverbs 27:15 says, "A continual dripping on a very rainy day / And a contentious woman are alike." Satan's accusations are like that—like a dripping faucet, or like a nagging wife—they will not let you go to sleep. But God's speaking is different. When you confess and claim the cleansing of the blood, God is instantly satisfied. Any further voice is Satan's.

If you confess your sin and claim the precious blood, yet some uneasiness continues to tug at you within, you should stop praying immediately. Do not confess anymore. Rather, turn to the source of the accusation and say something like this: "Satan, I have confessed my sin to God. He has forgiven my sin, and the blood of Jesus Christ has cleansed me from it. This uneasiness that I sense right now is not from God; it is from you, and I reject it! Satan, now you must look at the blood of Christ. That blood answers every one of your accusations." Try speaking to Satan in this way. When you use the blood in this way, Satan is defeated and he knows it. Revelation 12:10-11 says, "The accuser of our brothers has been cast down....And they overcame him because of the blood of the Lamb and because of the word of their testimony." The word of your testimony is just your declaration that the blood of Jesus Christ has cleansed you from every sin and that this blood has defeated Satan. When you speak boldly in this way, Satan's accusations are overcome.

The Christian life is a kind of warfare. Satan, "your adversary...as a roaring lion, walks about, seeking someone to devour" (1 Pet. 5:8). For this warfare, you need the proper weapons. One important weapon which you must utilize is the blood of Christ.

A DAILY LIFE
FULL OF GOD'S PRESENCE

By the power of the precious blood of Christ, it is possible for a Christian to live moment by moment in God's presence. Whenever any little sin would come to frustrate your fellowship with God, you may instantly confess and claim the Lord's prevailing blood. Immediately the fellowship is restored. Why should you waste time? The blood of Christ is available moment by moment, day after day. You can never exhaust the cleansing power of the blood of Christ. His blood is not only able to cleanse every past sin, but also every sin that you could ever commit.

By the power of the precious blood of Christ, you may enjoy a conscience free from the stain of guilt. Because of this, you can come boldly to God. "Let us come forward...with a true heart in full assurance of faith, having our hearts sprinkled from an evil conscience" (Heb. 10:22). By the blood of Christ, your conscience can be free from guilt. Like a freshly washed window, it can be clear, bright, and full of light.

Finally, by the power of the precious blood of Christ, you can overcome every accusation of Satan. Though his accusations may be strong, the blood of Christ is stronger. It answers them, every one. This blood is your weapon. With this weapon you could never be defeated by Satan; rather, he will be defeated by you.

How dear and how precious is the blood of Christ! By this blood you can live in God's presence day after day.

"If we walk in the light as He is in the light, we have fellowship with one another, and the blood of Jesus His Son cleanses us from every sin."
(1 John 1:7)